• The Human Body •

MUSCLES AND BONES

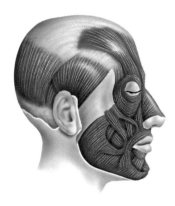

For a free color catalog describing Gareth Stevens' list of high-quality books and multimedia programs, call 1-800-542-2595 (USA) or 1-800-461-9120 (Canada). Gareth Stevens Publishing's Fax: (414) 225-0377. See our catalog, too, on the World Wide Web: gsinc.com

The editor would like to extend special thanks to Ronald J. Gerrits, Ph.D. (Physiology), Medical College of Wisconsin, Milwaukee, Wisconsin, for his kind and professional help with the information in this book.

Library of Congress Cataloging-in-Publication Data

Llamas, Andreu.
  [Músculos y los huesos. English]
  Muscles and bones / by Andreu Llamas ; illustrated by Luis Rizo.
    p. cm. — (The human body)
  Includes bibliographical references and index.
  Summary: Describes the human skeleton, major muscles of the body, the internal composition of bone, and the process of muscular contraction.
  ISBN 0-8368-2112-2 (lib. bdg.)
  1. Musculoskeletal system—Juvenile literature. [1. Muscular system. 2. Skeleton.]
I. Rizo, Luis, ill. II. Title. III. Series: Llamas, Andreu. The human body.
QP301.L6613   1998
612.7—dc21   98-6601

First published in North America in 1998 by
Gareth Stevens Publishing
1555 North RiverCenter Drive, Suite 201
Milwaukee, WI 53212 USA

This U.S. edition © 1998 by Gareth Stevens, Inc.
Original edition © 1996 by Ediciones Lema, S. L., Barcelona, Spain.
Additional end matter © 1998 by Gareth Stevens, Inc.

U. S. series editor: Rita Reitci
Editorial assistant: Diane Laska

Printed in Mexico

1 2 3 4 5 6 7 8 9 02 01 00 99 98

Gareth Stevens Publishing
MILWAUKEE

The Bones

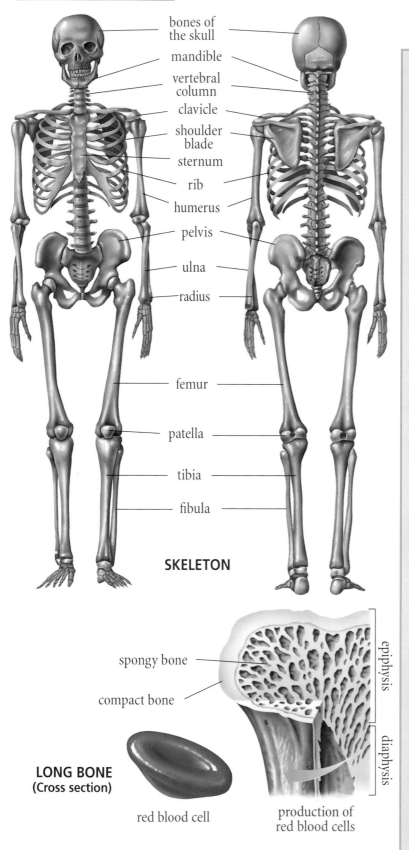

bones of the skull

mandible

vertebral column

clavicle

shoulder blade

sternum

rib

humerus

pelvis

ulna

radius

femur

patella

tibia

fibula

SKELETON

spongy bone

compact bone

LONG BONE
(Cross section)

red blood cell

epiphysis

diaphysis

production of red blood cells

A framework of bone. The locomotor system is a series of structures that allows your body to move. It is divided into three sections: skeleton, muscles, and joints.

The skeleton is the bony part of the body frame. It is made up of about 200 bones that give the body a hard structure to maintain its shape.

The human frame has three elements: the bones are the hard pieces that support the structures of the body; the muscles, more than 400, that move the bones and other organs; and the joints, which are places where two bones meet and are able to move. The bones consist of three parts: periosteum, osseous or bony substance, and bone marrow.

Bone structure. The periosteum is the outermost layer covering the exterior of the bones, except the areas of the joints. It contains nerves as well as blood vessels that bring nutrients to the bone.

The osseous, or bony, substance makes up the bone's hard part. It is formed of spongy bony tissue and compact bony tissue.

Bone marrow is a soft substance that fills the spaces of the spongy tissue. There are two kinds of bone marrow: red bone marrow and yellow bone marrow.

Red bone marrow produces blood cells, particularly the red blood cells. It is located in the center of short and flat bones and at the ends of long bones. Yellow bone marrow supports the red bone marrow, and reduces the weight of the bones. The shaft of long bones is called the diaphysis, and each end is known as an epiphysis. Growth of long bones takes place at the ends.

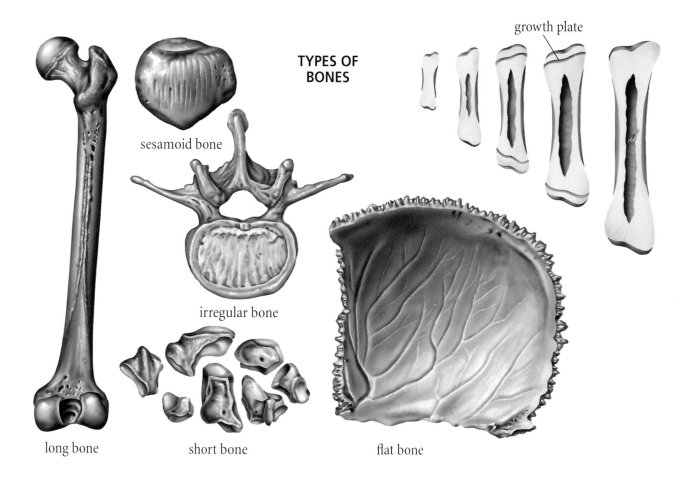

TYPES OF BONES

growth plate

sesamoid bone

irregular bone

long bone

short bone

flat bone

Uses. Besides supporting the body, the bones have other important functions. They protect the main organs, such as the heart, the lungs, and the brain. Red bone marrow produces red blood cells, white blood cells, and blood platelets.

Bone stores excess minerals, such as calcium and phosphorus. These minerals are released when needed by the body. Calcium is essential for blood clotting and muscle contraction.

Growth. Although bones start to form in the fetus, at birth they are not calcified. Instead, they are composed of cartilage, which is a more elastic tissue. This cartilage enables the bones to keep growing until we become adults.

During growth, bone keeps calcifying and hardening. At the same time, the bone grows longer at the growing plate, or epiphyseal disk, near each end. Epiphyseal disk cartilage ossifies completely at 16-25 years of age, marking the end of bone growth.

The shapes of bones. Bone shapes can be long, such as the femur and humerus; flat, such as the ribs, skull bones, and shoulder blade; short, such as the carpus of the wrist; or irregular, such as vertebrae, auditory ossicles, and sesamoids. The patella, or kneecap, is a sesamoid bone.

A long bone, such as the femur, consists of the shaft, or diaphysis, and two ends, the epiphyses. The diaphysis has a central, or medullary, cavity containing yellow bone marrow. Flat bones have two compact layers, or laminae, with spongy tissue between. Short bones are made up of spongy bone tissue surrounded by a layer of compact bone.

The Muscles

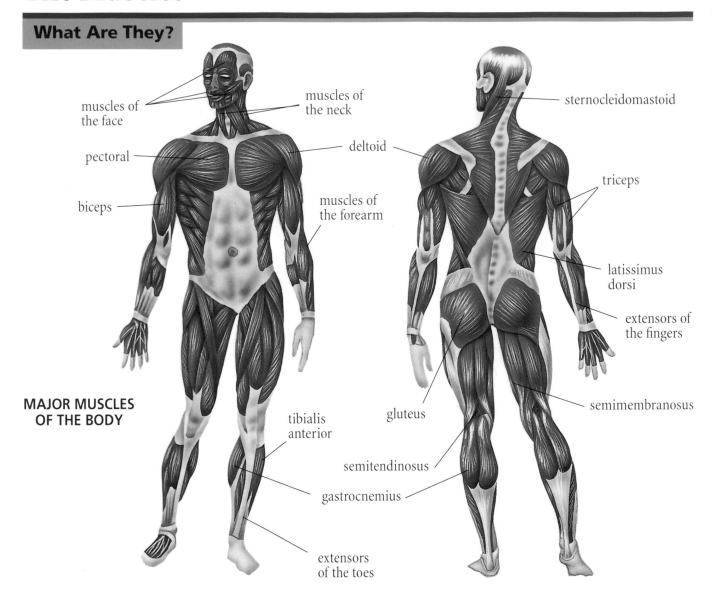

muscles of the face

muscles of the neck

sternocleidomastoid

pectoral

deltoid

triceps

biceps

muscles of the forearm

latissimus dorsi

extensors of the fingers

MAJOR MUSCLES OF THE BODY

tibialis anterior

gluteus

semimembranosus

semitendinosus

gastrocnemius

extensors of the toes

Muscle power. Muscles power the locomotor system, following instructions from the nerves. Muscles constitute between 35-40 percent of the body's total weight. There are more than 400 muscles in the body, although some of them are small and have little power. This large number of muscles is needed to carry out various kinds of coordinated movements.

Muscles are in contact with many different structures in the body. They are attached to bones, either directly or by a tendon; to skin, such as the muscles of the face; and to the mucosae, such as the muscles that move the tongue.

Types of muscles. There are three kinds of muscles: long, wide, and short. The long muscles are located in the arms and legs, where they cause wide and fast movements of these limbs.

Wide muscles are flat and thin. They are located on the walls of the thorax and the abdomen. There, they provide a wide and powerful lining to both the thoracic cavity and the abdominal cavity.

Short muscles are small and in different shapes. They do not move very much, but they are very powerful. For instance, many short muscles surround the spinal cord.

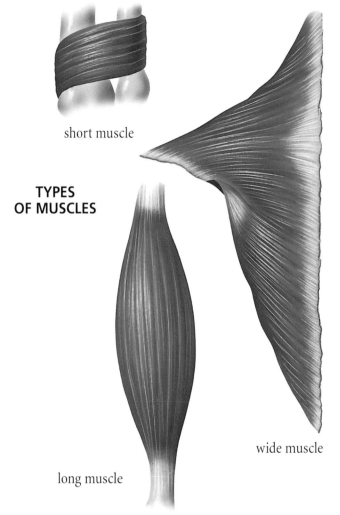

TYPES OF MUSCLES

short muscle

long muscle

wide muscle

Muscle contraction. Muscles contract when they receive an impulse from a nerve.

Muscle is made up of little muscular fibers that contain hundreds or thousands of myofibrils. Each myofibril is composed of thousands of contracting units. Each of the units is made up of two proteins — actin and myosin. The centers of the contracting units contain filaments of myosin, whose ends are inserted within filaments of actin.

When stimulated by a nerve impulse, the actin filaments move closer to one another over the myosin filaments. This reduces the distance between them, producing muscle contraction. When the muscle relaxes, the actin molecules move back to their resting position.

Muscles at rest. When muscles are at rest, they show a state of contraction known as muscle tone. Muscle tone is responsible for your posture — even when you are asleep!

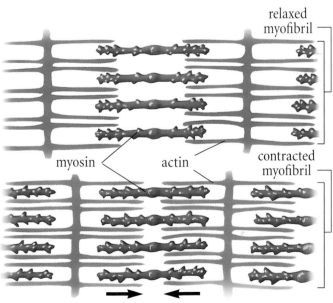

relaxed myofibril

myosin

actin

contracted myofibril

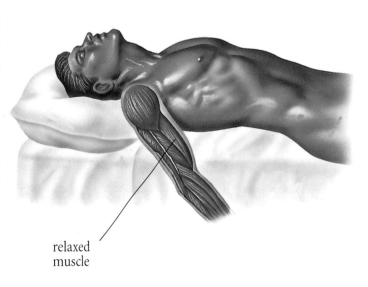

relaxed muscle

The Bones of the Skull

What Are They?

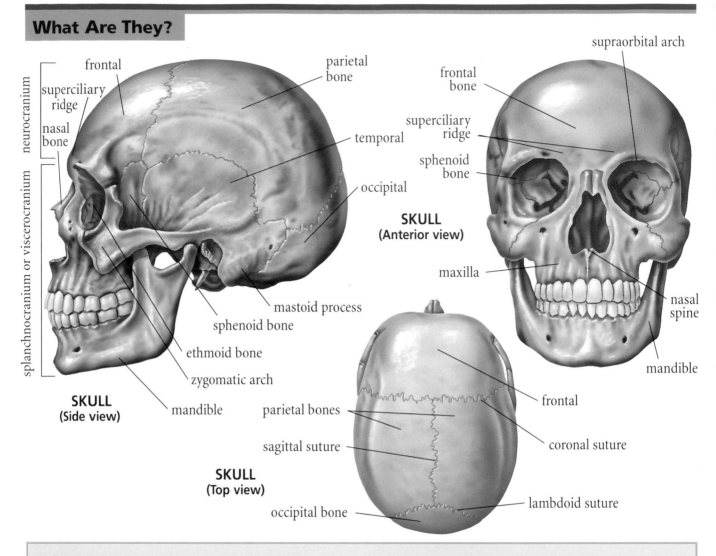

neurocranium

splanchnocranium or viscerocranium

frontal

superciliary ridge

nasal bone

parietal bone

temporal

occipital

mastoid process

sphenoid bone

ethmoid bone

zygomatic arch

mandible

SKULL
(Side view)

supraorbital arch

frontal bone

superciliary ridge

sphenoid bone

maxilla

nasal spine

mandible

SKULL
(Anterior view)

frontal

coronal suture

parietal bones

sagittal suture

lambdoid suture

occipital bone

SKULL
(Top view)

Bones that protect. The skull has 22 bones joined together to protect the brain, eyes, and ears. The bones of the skull can be divided into two parts: the eight bones of the neurocranium, which protects the brain; and the 14 bones of the splanchnocranium, or viscerocranium, which forms the face.

The bones making up the neurocranium are: two parietals, two temporals, a frontal, an occipital, an ethmoid, and a sphenoid. These bones fit together in immovable joints called sutures.

A newborn has areas, called fontanels, between the bones of its skull that are filled with fibrous connective tissue. These are often called "soft spots." They allow the cranium to be squeezed as it passes through the birth canal. By the age of two, the fontanels have filled in with bone.

The flat bones of the skull are formed by inner and outer laminae, or layers, of compact bone. The laminae are separated by a layer of spongy bone, called diploe. Besides protecting the brain, the skull structurally supports the face and houses the first sections of the respiratory and digestive systems.

The temporals are complicated bones. They form the two sides of the skull and contain channels leading to the middle and inner ear.

The smallest bones in the body are in the middle ear: malleus, incus, and stapes. These transmit sound vibrations from the eardrum to the inner ear.

The frontal bone curves up to form the forehead and the upper part of the orbits, which are deep bone cavities in which the eyes are located. The mandible is the only movable bone of the skull.

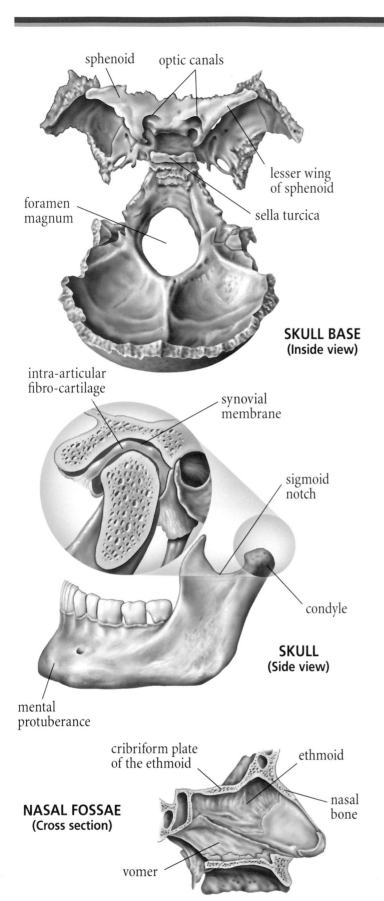

sphenoid optic canals

lesser wing of sphenoid

foramen magnum

sella turcica

SKULL BASE
(Inside view)

intra-articular fibro-cartilage

synovial membrane

sigmoid notch

condyle

SKULL
(Side view)

mental protuberance

cribriform plate of the ethmoid

ethmoid

nasal bone

NASAL FOSSAE
(Cross section)

vomer

Base of skull. A bottom view of the skull shows two bones: the irregular sphenoid and the flat occipital.

The sphenoid has two big wings. It forms part of the base of the skull and supports the other cranial bones. Its unique shape allows the sphenoid to fit with the rest of the cranial bones.

The occipital bone is located on the back of the skull, at the base. The lower part of the occipital bears a large opening called the foramen magnum, or occipital hole. The spinal cord runs through the foramen magnum to join the brain.

Lower jaw. The mandible, or lower jaw, is a strong, curved bone that contains the lower teeth. The maxilla, or upper jaw, contains the upper teeth. The mandible moves against the maxilla so that both sets of teeth bite and chew.

The temporomandibular joint between the jaw and the temporal bone is unique. The condyle at the head of the mandible is almost cylindrical. It fits in such a way that when you open your mouth, there is a circular motion in the lower joint and a sliding motion in the upper one. Lateral, or sideways, movements can also occur.

Nasal cavities. The ethmoid is a small bone that is part of the nasal fossae, or cavities. There are two fossae, separated by the nasal septum. Part of the ethmoid is pierced with small holes to form the cribriform plate of the ethmoid. Through these run branches of the olfactory nerve, carrying odor sensations to the brain. The vomer, a single upright bone, forms part of the nasal septum.

The Muscles of the Head

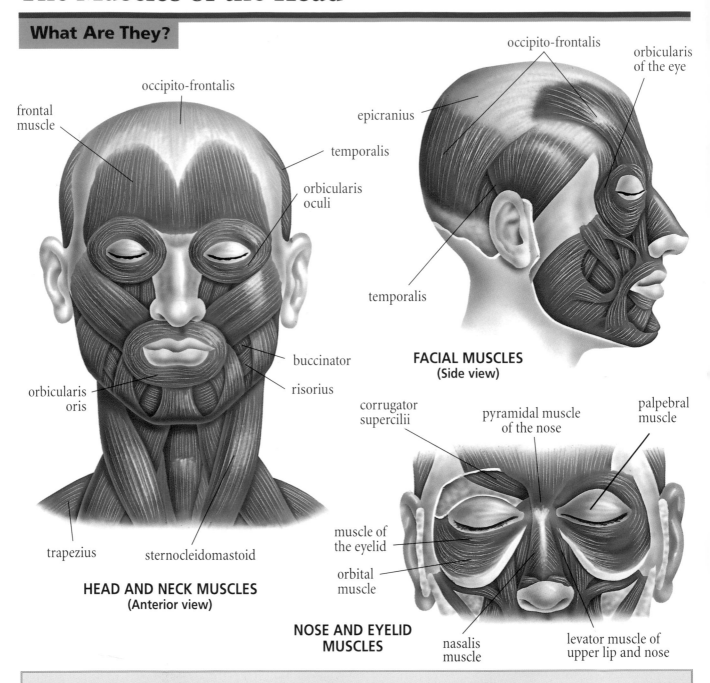

FACIAL MUSCLES
(Side view)

frontal muscle

occipito-frontalis

temporalis

orbicularis oculi

orbicularis oris

trapezius

sternocleidomastoid

buccinator

risorius

HEAD AND NECK MUSCLES
(Anterior view)

occipito-frontalis

epicranius

orbicularis of the eye

temporalis

corrugator supercilii

pyramidal muscle of the nose

palpebral muscle

muscle of the eyelid

orbital muscle

nasalis muscle

levator muscle of upper lip and nose

NOSE AND EYELID MUSCLES

Expressions. Generally, the muscles of the head are small and of two main types: the facial, or mimicry, muscles and the mastication, or chewing, muscles.

The muscles involved in facial expressions are in the following groups: muscles of the vault of the cranium; muscles of the palpebral, or eyelid, area; muscles of the nasal area; and muscles of the buccal, or mouth, area. The facial muscles are in contact with the bones and the skin in the face. When these muscles contract, they cause the skin to fold in several lines, resulting in various facial expressions. When the skin is young and elastic, the wrinkles caused by the muscular contractions disappear. However, as we grow older, the skin loses its elasticity, and then the wrinkles become permanent.

The function of the mastication, or chewing, muscles is to break down food so that ingestion and digestion are easier. The masseter, for example, is a very powerful muscle. It can move the jaw with a strength equivalent to 220 pounds (100 kilograms)!

LOWER FACE MUSCLES

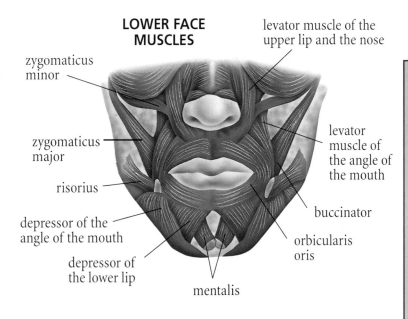

zygomaticus minor

levator muscle of the upper lip and the nose

zygomaticus major

levator muscle of the angle of the mouth

risorius

buccinator

depressor of the angle of the mouth

orbicularis oris

depressor of the lower lip

mentalis

temporalis

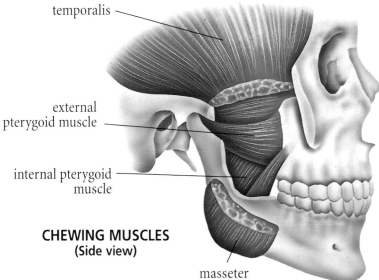

external pterygoid muscle

internal pterygoid muscle

CHEWING MUSCLES
(Side view)

masseter

omohyoid

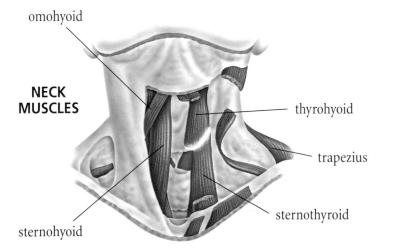

NECK MUSCLES

thyrohyoid

trapezius

sternothyroid

sternohyoid

Head and neck. The sternocleidomastoid muscle rotates and extends the head.

Upper face. The epicranius lifts the upper eyelids and the eyebrows to express surprise. The occipital lifts the eyebrows. The temporalis tightens the scalp.

Nose and eyes. The orbital and palpebral, muscles of the eyes, produce worried expressions. The pyramidal of the nose produces a threatening expression. The nasal muscles express surprise, joy, desire, and demand. The muscles that lift the upper lip and the nose express astonishment and bad temper.

Lower face. The orbicular muscle in the lips contracts to bring the lips together to suck and drink. The buccinator expels air from the mouth and acts when you cry and laugh. The zygomatic produces expressions of pleasure and skepticism. This muscle is responsible for laughter. Other muscles act when you express self-confidence (levator muscle of the mouth), sadness (depressor of the angle of the mouth), firmness (depressor of the lower lip and the nose), and doubt (mentalis).

Chewing. Mastication muscles move the mandible, or lower jaw. The masseter lifts the mandible to close the mouth and grind the teeth in chewing. The temporalis is the most powerful jaw-lifter. The external pterygoid controls the joint of the jaw in all its movements. The internal pterygoid lifts and rotates the jaw, moving it forward and sideways.

Neck. Thick and powerful neck muscles cover and protect the bones joining the head and the trunk. They allow the head to go through a wide range of movements.

The Bones of the Upper Limbs

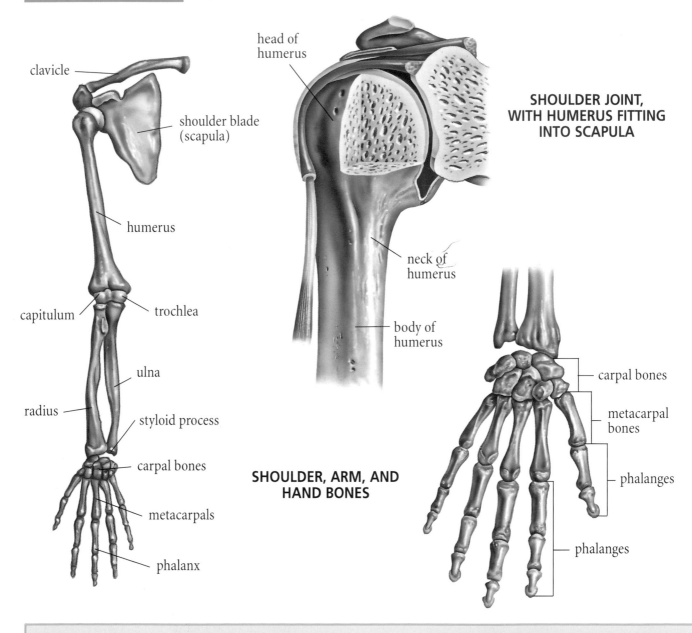

clavicle

shoulder blade (scapula)

head of humerus

SHOULDER JOINT, WITH HUMERUS FITTING INTO SCAPULA

humerus

neck of humerus

body of humerus

capitulum

trochlea

ulna

radius

styloid process

carpal bones

metacarpal bones

phalanges

carpal bones

SHOULDER, ARM, AND HAND BONES

metacarpals

phalanx

phalanges

Arms and hands. Each upper limb has a shoulder, arm, forearm, and hand. The shoulder is located in the upper part of the thorax and consists of two bones: the scapula, or shoulder blade, at the back; and the clavicle, or collarbone, at the front. The clavicle is shaped like an S. One end attaches to the sternum and the other end to the scapula. Joints at each end allow complicated movements of the shoulder. The shoulder blade, or scapula, is long, flat, and triangular. The collarbone, or clavicle, anchors many ligaments and muscles.

The humerus is a long, cylindrical bone in the upper arm. Its smooth, rounded top fits into the joint of the shoulder blade. At its lower end, the humerus meets the radius and the ulna to form the elbow joint.

The forearm has two long parallel bones, the radius and the ulna, which allow the wrist to turn.

The hand contains 27 small bones between the wrist and the fingertips. These are grouped into carpals, metacarpals, and phalanges. They allow the hand flexibility to perform numerous tasks.

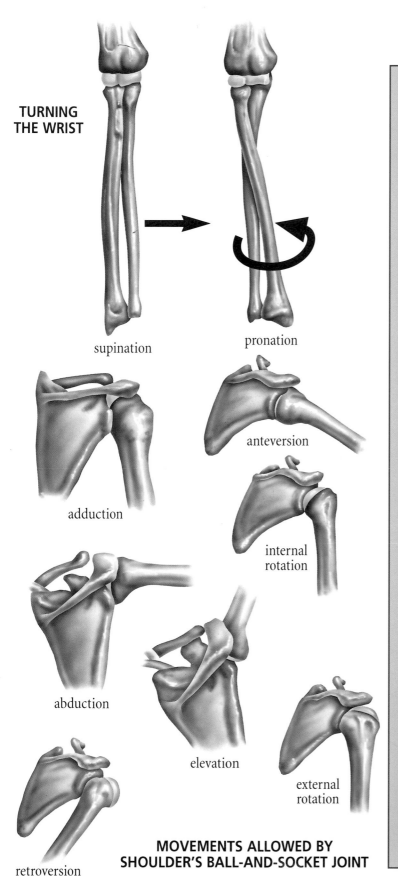

TURNING THE WRIST

supination

pronation

adduction

anteversion

abduction

internal rotation

elevation

external rotation

retroversion

MOVEMENTS ALLOWED BY SHOULDER'S BALL-AND-SOCKET JOINT

The bones of the arm make possible a wide range of movement.

Wrist twist. The ulna hinges with the humerus at the elbow. In rotating the wrist in pronation (palm down), the radius crosses the ulna, forming an X. The X uncrosses during supination (palm up).

Many movements. The ball-and-socket joint formed by the head of the humerus and the shoulder blade allows a great degree of movement in nearly every direction.

Abduction and adduction. Abduction is the act of moving the entire arm away from the side of the body until it points straight out at a 90° angle. Adduction takes place when the arm moves back down to the body's side. Elevation is the continuation of abduction, with the head of the humerus rotating at the shoulder joint, until the arm is completely upright.

Lifting and rotating. Anteversion is the forward lifting of an arm, as in pointing at something. Retroversion occurs when you lift the arm backward. Rotation takes place when the arm swings around a line formed by the head of the humerus and the styloid of the ulna. External rotation moves the head of the humerus outward in its socket, and internal rotation moves the humerus head inward.

Grasping. The wrist and hand contain 27 bones. The eight carpals of the wrist are placed in two rows of four. Five metacarpals brace the back of the hand. Each finger has three phalanges, except the thumb. The thumb has only two phalanges. The position of the opposable thumb allows it to touch the other fingers. This grasping ability enables humans to use tools.

The Muscles of the Upper Limbs

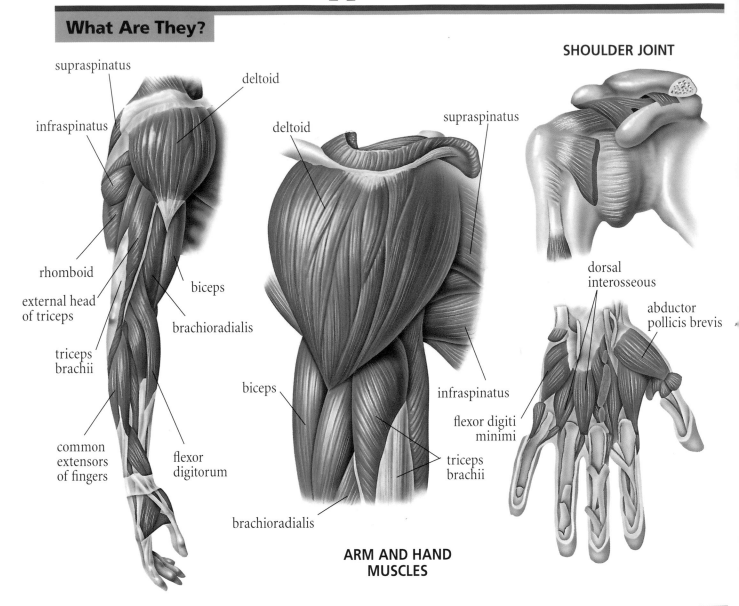

SHOULDER JOINT

supraspinatus

deltoid

infraspinatus

rhomboid

external head of triceps

triceps brachii

common extensors of fingers

biceps

brachioradialis

flexor digitorum

deltoid

supraspinatus

biceps

infraspinatus

flexor digiti minimi

triceps brachii

brachioradialis

dorsal interosseous

abductor pollicis brevis

ARM AND HAND MUSCLES

Moving arms and hands. The muscles of the upper limbs are grouped into four areas: shoulder muscles, upper arm muscles, forearm muscles, and hand muscles.

There are six muscles in the shoulder. These are: deltoid, infraspinatus, supraspinatus, teres major, teres minor, and subscapular. Together, they allow the shoulder a wide range of movement.

The deltoid muscle covers the shoulder. This muscle is the main abductor of the arm. It is the only muscle that can raise the arm 90°. When this muscle contracts, it pulls up the arm until the limb is held straight out from the side.

The upper arm has muscles both in front and in back. The muscles located in front are the brachial biceps, brachioradialis, and brachialis. The back of the upper arm is the site of the triceps.

Located in the forearm are the flexors and extensors of the fingers. These muscles move the fingers. The palm of the hand contains 19 muscles in all. These hand muscles are small and short because their only job is to move the fingers.

The abductor pollicis brevis allows the thumb to oppose the fingers. Because thumb and fingers work together to grasp objects, humans can perform complex, delicate maneuvers and manipulate tools.

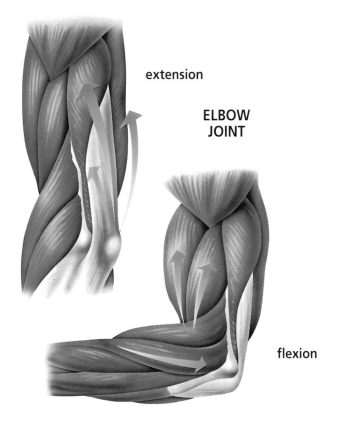

extension

ELBOW JOINT

flexion

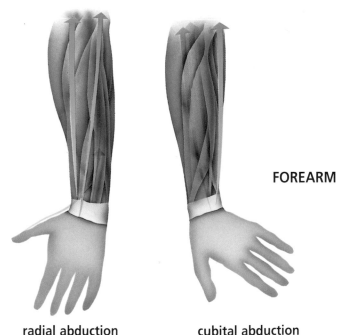

FOREARM

radial abduction

cubital abduction

The elbow joint. Two main muscles of the arm, the biceps and the triceps, have opposite actions. Muscles paired, or complemented, in this way are called antagonist muscles. The biceps helps the forearm to flex, or bend toward the upper arm. Its antagonist, the triceps, contracts to extend, or straighten out, the forearm.

The elbow joint is built like a hinge, and extension and flexion are simple up and down, or forward and back, movements. The muscles in front of the hinge, or elbow, are flexors. The ones below the hinge, or in back of the elbow, are extensors.

The forearm. The supinator muscles and the pronator muscles of the forearm perform a wide range of movements: rotating the forearm, moving the hand in all directions, and extending the fingers. The supinator muscles turn the palm up in a movement called radial abduction. The pronators turn the palm down, in a movement known as cubital abduction. Bending the hand upward is called dorsi flexion, and bending it downward is called palmaris flexion.

Every time a muscle contracts, its complementary antagonist stretches.

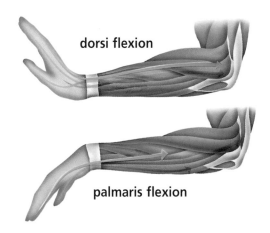

dorsi flexion

palmaris flexion

The Bones of the Lower Limbs

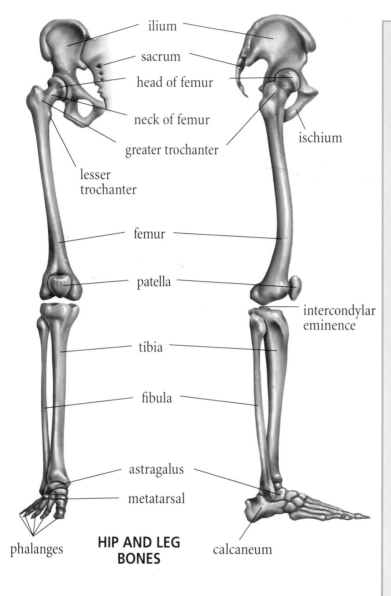

ilium
sacrum
head of femur
neck of femur
greater trochanter
lesser trochanter
ischium
femur
patella
intercondylar eminence
tibia
fibula
astragalus
metatarsal
phalanges
calcaneum

HIP AND LEG BONES

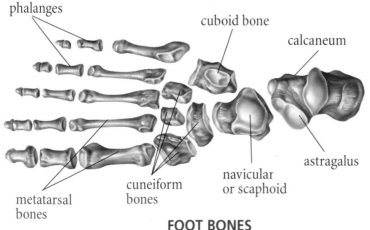

phalanges
cuboid bone
calcaneum
navicular or scaphoid
astragalus
cuneiform bones
metatarsal bones

FOOT BONES

Bones for walking and running. The leg has the following bones: femur, tibia, fibula, patella, and the bones of the foot.

The femur is the longest bone in the body. It is also one of the thickest and strongest. Its upper end consists of head, neck, and trochanters, or bony processes that add leverage to the muscles rotating the thigh.

The neck of the femur is a narrow area just below the head. This area is subjected to a great deal of force. The diaphysis of the femur is very long and sturdy.

The patella, or kneecap, is the biggest sesamoid bone in the body. It is short, round, and flat, and roughly triangular in shape, with the base up and the point down. The patella protects the knee joint.

The tibia in the lower leg is a long and sturdy bone that supports most of the body's weight. Its upper end joins the femur, and its lower end joins with the bones of the ankle. It also joins laterally with the fibula, a long bone thinner and less strong than the tibia.

Flexible foot. The foot contains 7 short bones and 19 long bones, divided into tarsus, metatarsus, and phalanges.

The bones of the tarsus are: astragalus, calcaneum, navicular or scaphoid, cuboid, and cuneiform bones.

The metatarsus has five metatarsal bones. Every toe has three phalanges, except the big toe, which has only two phalanges.

The astragalus joins the tibia and the fibula with the foot. This bone transmits the weight of the body to the foot. The calcaneum is the biggest and sturdiest bone in the foot. It forms the heel.

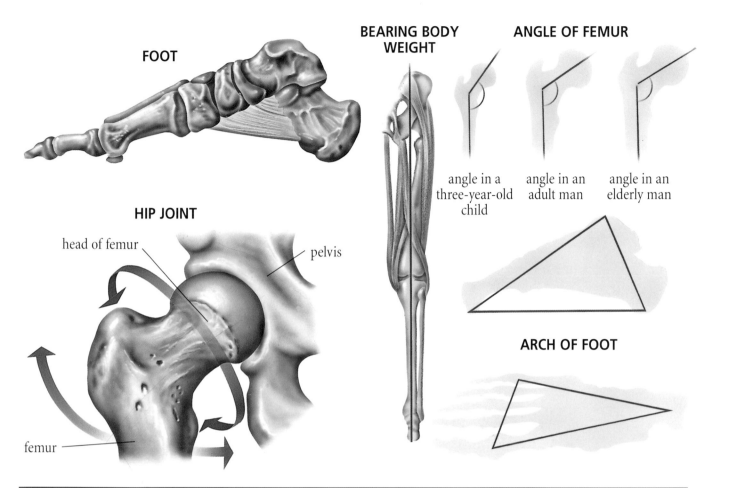

FOOT

BEARING BODY WEIGHT

ANGLE OF FEMUR

angle in a three-year-old child

angle in an adult man

angle in an elderly man

HIP JOINT

head of femur

pelvis

femur

ARCH OF FOOT

The foot. The foot has a great number of joints that support the weight of the body. Because of this, most of the joint faces are flat, with ligaments that are short and very strong. Besides supporting the weight of the body, the ligaments maintain the position of the bones in the arch. If there is a weakness in any ligament, the arch may drop. This condition is called fallen arch, or flat foot.

The toes have joints just like the fingers, but these are less developed and have much less movement. The calcaneum and the arch form a shock absorber to cushion the foot from the impact of every step.

The hip joint. The spherical, smooth-walled head of the femur fits into the hip joint cavity. This ball-and-socket joint can move in all directions. Cartilage between ball and socket protects both from wear.

Angle of femur. The body and the neck of the femur form an angle that becomes narrower during growth. It is about 130° in an average adult man. In women and shorter individuals, the angle can be narrower. The angle stabilizes the body, supporting its entire weight whenever humans stand.

Bearing weight. When the leg is healthy and the knee works properly, the line that supports the weight of the body passes through the midpoint of the head of the femur, the midpoint of the knee joint, and the midpoint of the calcaneum. This balanced support avoids risk of overloading and eventually damaging these structures.

Three-point support. The foot's arch supports the weight of the body on three bony points. Two points are in the metatarsal area; the third is the calcaneum.

The Muscles of the Lower Limbs

What Are They?

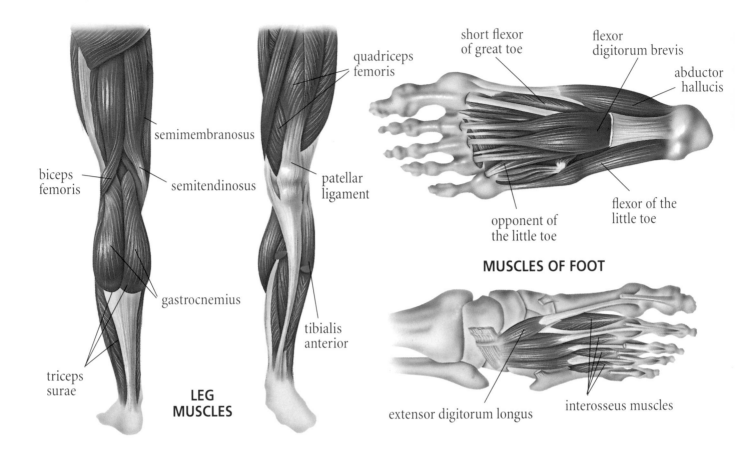

quadriceps femoris

semimembranosus

biceps femoris

semitendinosus

patellar ligament

gastrocnemius

tibialis anterior

triceps surae

LEG MUSCLES

short flexor of great toe

flexor digitorum brevis

abductor hallucis

opponent of the little toe

flexor of the little toe

MUSCLES OF FOOT

extensor digitorum longus

interosseus muscles

Leg muscles. The muscles in the legs are long so they can make wide and fast movements. The lower limbs' important muscles are: quadriceps femoris, semimembranosus, semitendinosus, biceps femoris, large and short adductors, tibialis anterior, extensor digitorum longus, and gastrocnemius.

The quadriceps muscle is made up of four sections: rectus femoris, vastus medialis, vastus lateralis, and vastus intermedius. These attach to the femur and the hip bone. At the lower end, they join each other to form the patellar ligament (that covers the patella), which anchors on the front of the upper tibia. The quadriceps is a very powerful muscle, which is responsible for stretching the leg.

The upper ends of the adductors attach to the pelvis and the lower ends to the femur. These muscles move the thigh closer to the midline of the body.

The semimembranosus, the semitendinosus, and the biceps femoris muscles are at the back of the thigh. Their upper ends attach to the femur and the ischium of the pelvis. The lower ends insert in the tibia and the fibula. The job of these muscles is to flex the leg. The tibialis anterior lifts the foot upward (dorsal flexion), and the extensors of the toes straighten these digits.

The triceps surae is formed by the gastrocnemius and the soleus muscles. The upper ends of the gastrocnemius insert in the lower end of the femur. The soleus inserts in the back of the tibia and the fibula. The lower tendon is common to these muscles and is called the Achilles tendon. It is attached to the calcaneum.

The triceps muscles help extend the foot, move the foot forward, and support the weight of the body.

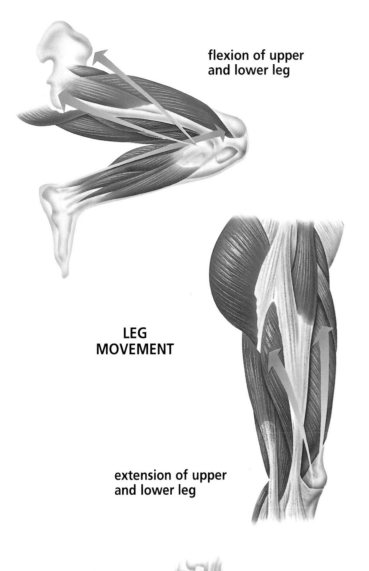

flexion of upper
and lower leg

**LEG
MOVEMENT**

extension of upper
and lower leg

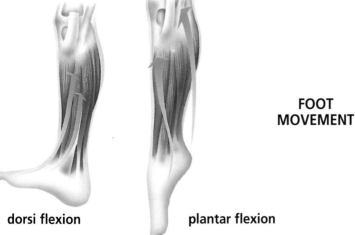

dorsi flexion

plantar flexion

**FOOT
MOVEMENT**

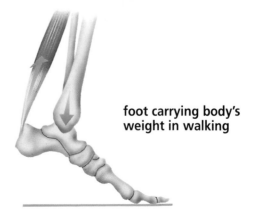

foot carrying body's
weight in walking

A system of levers for moving. The movements of the human body result from the contraction of muscles acting on the system of levers formed by the bones and joints. For this reason, the muscles in the legs need to be very strong and powerful. They control the entire body when it is moving across a distance.

Leg movement. The extension of the leg is due to the contraction of the quadriceps femoris. The quadriceps becomes more powerful when the hip is extended.

Flexion of the leg is due to the action of several different muscles. These include the sartorius, gracilis, biceps femoris, popliteus, semimembranosus, semitendinosus, and gastrocnemius.

Foot movement in walking. In order to walk correctly, muscles move each foot in dorsal flexion and plantar flexion. If these muscles did not work properly, the foot could not make the necessary movements for walking and running.

The foot must be strong enough to bear the weight of the body, yet flexible enough to act as a lever in propelling the body forward. This design enables us to walk with minimum effort.

The Spine

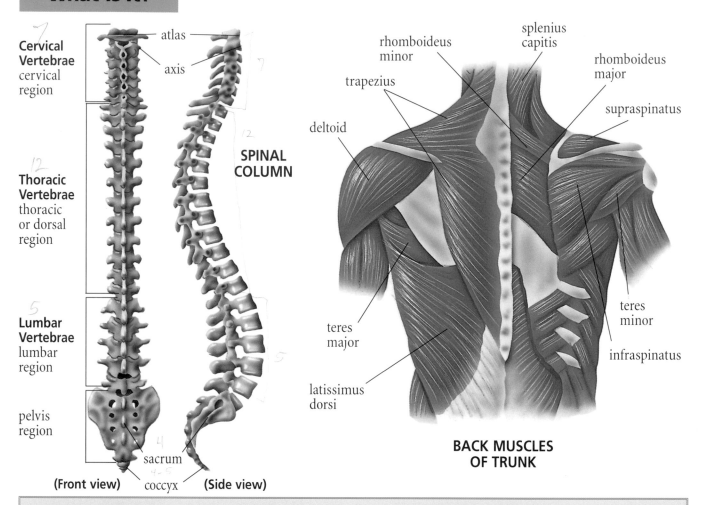

Cervical Vertebrae
cervical region

atlas

axis

Thoracic Vertebrae
thoracic or dorsal region

SPINAL COLUMN

Lumbar Vertebrae
lumbar region

pelvis region

sacrum

coccyx

(Front view) **(Side view)**

rhomboideus minor

splenius capitis

rhomboideus major

trapezius

deltoid

supraspinatus

teres major

teres minor

infraspinatus

latissimus dorsi

BACK MUSCLES OF TRUNK

Flexible support. The spine that supports the human body has 33-34 vertebrae, bound together by muscles and ligaments. The vertebrae are separated by intervertebral discs of cartilage. The spine encloses the spinal cord.

Every vertebra has a central hole called the spinal foramen. All of these together form the spinal canal, through which the spinal cord runs. Small projections, or processes, on the vertebrae allow muscles to attach. The top of the spine articulates with the occipital bone of the skull. This bone bears the foramen magnum, through which the spinal cord connects with the brain. The lower end of the spine attaches to the sacrum, and the sacrum joins the coccyx.

The spine has five divisions: cervical spine, thoracic spine, lumbar spine, sacrum, and coccyx.

The cervical area, located in the neck, consists of seven thin, movable cervical vertebrae. The first vertebra is called the atlas. It is ring-shaped and bears the weight of the head. The second is the axis, which allows the head to rotate from side to side.

The thoracic area consists of 12 thoracic vertebrae that are larger and less movable than the cervical.

The lumbar area, in the lower back, has five lumbar vertebrae. They are the largest and strongest and occupy the lowest position of the movable vertebrae.

The pelvic area contains nine or ten vertebrae. Five are sacral vertebrae that are fused to form the sacrum. This is a very sturdy bone that forms the base of the spinal column. The four or five remaining vertebrae are the coccygeal, fused to form the coccyx, to which some muscles attach.

SCALENUS MUSCLES

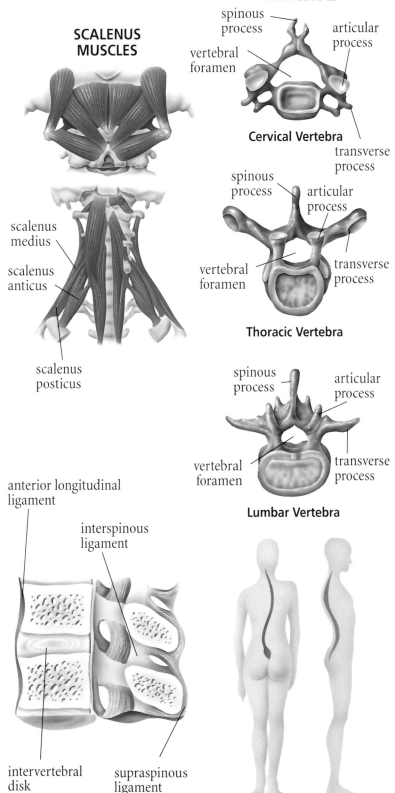

scalenus medius

scalenus anticus

scalenus posticus

TYPES OF VERTEBRAE

spinous process

vertebral foramen

articular process

Cervical Vertebra

transverse process

spinous process

articular process

vertebral foramen

transverse process

Thoracic Vertebra

spinous process

articular process

vertebral foramen

transverse process

Lumbar Vertebra

anterior longitudinal ligament

interspinous ligament

intervertebral disk

supraspinous ligament

INTERVERTEBRAL DISKS

DEVIATIONS OF SPINE

Spine. The vertebral column seen from back or front is completely straight. But a side view shows the curvatures needed to maintain the body's natural erect posture. The column's sturdy and flexible structures keep the vertebrae aligned to prevent displacement. Abnormal spinal curvatures, or deviations, can result from disease or chronic poor posture.

Trunk muscles. The back muscles of the trunk keep the head and the vertebral column erect and also help the shoulders move. Their continuous contraction keeps the body erect, without being pulled forward by the weight of internal organs.

Scalenus muscles. The front, middle, and back scalenus muscles pull the first two ribs upward during inhalation. This movement expands the upper thorax to enable air to enter.

Vertebrae. Vertebrae are short bones with soft bony tissue inside them. Each has two parts: the body at the front, and the processes in back and on the sides. Between them is the vertebral foramen, or spinal hole, about 1 inch (2-4 centimeters) in diameter, which allows the spinal cord to pass through it. Unlike other vertebrae, the atlas (first vertebra) lacks a body, but it has a round edge that fits with the axis to enable the head to move.

Invertebral disks. The 23 spinal disks are flat laminae with a sturdy fibrous outer ring and a soft, gelatinous nucleus. The disks allow the movements of flexion and extension, lateral motion, and rotation of the vertebral column. They also act as shock absorbers. The disks in the lumbar region are much thicker than the others.

The Bones of the Thoracic Cage

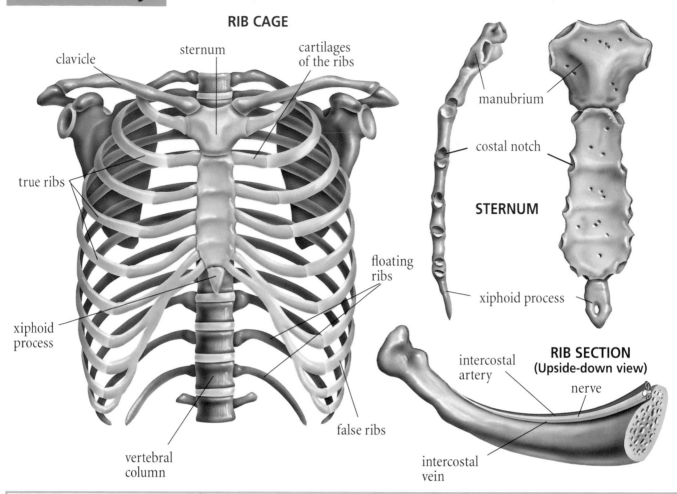

RIB CAGE

clavicle
sternum
cartilages of the ribs
true ribs
floating ribs
xiphoid process
false ribs
vertebral column

manubrium
costal notch

STERNUM

xiphoid process

RIB SECTION
(Upside-down view)
intercostal artery
nerve
intercostal vein

A cage of bone. The rib, or thoracic, cage protects the heart and lungs. It consists of the thoracic vertebrae, the sternum, and 12 pairs of ribs.

The ribs are long, flat bones. Each rib begins at a thoracic vertebra and curves around to the front. The curve is continued by a long piece of costal cartilage that attaches to the sternum. The end of the cartilage fits into a depression, called the costal icisura, in the long edge of the sternum.

Two ribs arise from each of the 12 thoracic vertebrae, one for each side of the body, for a total of 24 ribs. Sometimes there is an extra rib.

The first seven pairs of ribs are called true ribs, for they are directly connected to the sternum. The last five pairs are known as false ribs, for they do not attach to the sternum. Of these, the first three pairs of false ribs have their cartilages connected to the cartilage of the rib above them. The last two pairs of ribs are called floating ribs because their cartilages end in the muscle in the abdominal wall. Arteries and veins, as well as the nerves of the thoracic wall, run under every rib.

The sternum (breastbone) is a flat bone 6-8 inches (15-20 cm) long. It has two layers of compact tissue, separated by a layer of spongy tissue. The clavicles and the first seven ribs are attached on each side to this tissue.

The structure at the top of the sternum is known as the manubrium. The small part at the bottom of the sternum is called the xiphoid process. The sternum's long edges bear seven pairs of costal incisurae, or notches, to receive the first seven ribs.

sternoclavicular joint

STERNUM AND RIB JOINTS

sternum

ribs

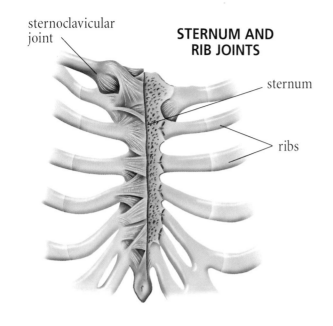

VERTEBRAE AND RIB JOINTS

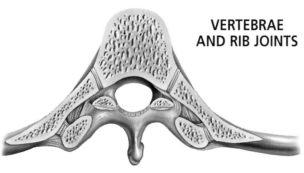

VERTEBRAE AND RIBS
(Cross section)

costotransverse ligaments

ribs

anterior longitudinal ligament

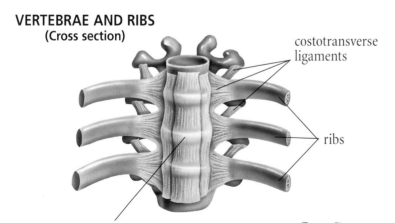

Sternum and rib joints. The sternum forms joints with the clavicle and the ribs. The sternoclavicular joint allows for various movements of the shoulder. For this, the clavicle attaches to the upper sternum with interclavicular ligaments and other ligaments lying between the ribs and the clavicle. These ligaments allow the ribs to expand and contract during respiratory movements.

Vertebrae and rib joints. The joints attaching ribs to the vertebral column allow the ribs to raise and lower.

Rib motion is crucial for respiration. This is made possible by joints between the ribs, between the ribs and the vertebrae, and between the ribs and the sternum.

Thorax in motion. The elasticity of the thorax gives it strength and allows the movements needed for respiration.

When you inhale, the thorax enlarges. The ribs move at their joints with the vertebrae. The elastic costal cartilage at the front ends of the ribs allows the rib cage to expand. The curve in the spinal column increases. This expansion results in increased volume that allows air to enter the lungs.

When you exhale, the ribs lower to their resting position. The thorax decreases in size, reducing its volume. This pushes air out of the lungs.

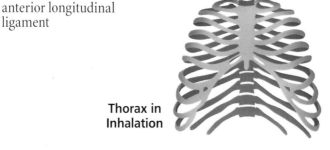

Thorax in Inhalation

BREATHING MOVEMENTS OF THORAX

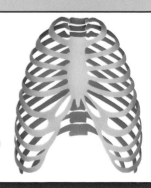

Thorax in Exhalation

The Muscles of the Thorax and the Abdomen

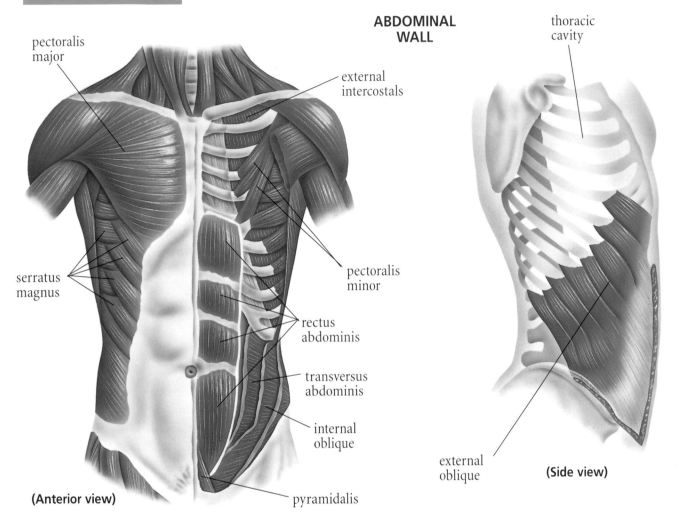

ABDOMINAL WALL

thoracic cavity

pectoralis major

external intercostals

serratus magnus

pectoralis minor

rectus abdominis

transversus abdominis

internal oblique

external oblique

(Side view)

(Anterior view)

pyramidalis

Trunk muscles. The thoracic muscles are wide, flat, and relatively thin. The pectoral, the outermost muscle, is triangular, has a large surface, and attaches to the clavicle, sternum, and ribs. It ends in a tendon that inserts into the humerus, making the upper arm rotate and lower.

The pectoralis minor has three separate tendons inserted into the first ribs. Its fibers go upward to connect with the tendon that attaches to the scapula. In respiration, the pectoralis minor pulls the ribs upward when the scapula is not moving. It also helps move the upper arm and the shoulder.

The serratus anterior connects the first nine ribs with the scapula; it also assists in respiration and in respiratory movements.

The serratus posterior pulls the ribs upward, and the lower serratus posterior lowers them. The muscle is long and divided because of the presence of tendinous segments. It inserts into the sternum and the ribs, with its lower end attached to the coxal, or innominate, bone of the pubis. It helps the pelvis bend back and forth on the trunk. As a respiratory muscle, it helps in exhaling.

The abdominal fibers of the various muscle layers run in different directions. This arrangement provides maximum strength and protection. The muscles are in three groups. The lateral group: external oblique, internal oblique, and transversal; the medial group: pyramidal and rectus; and the deep group: lumbar quadratus and psoas magnus.

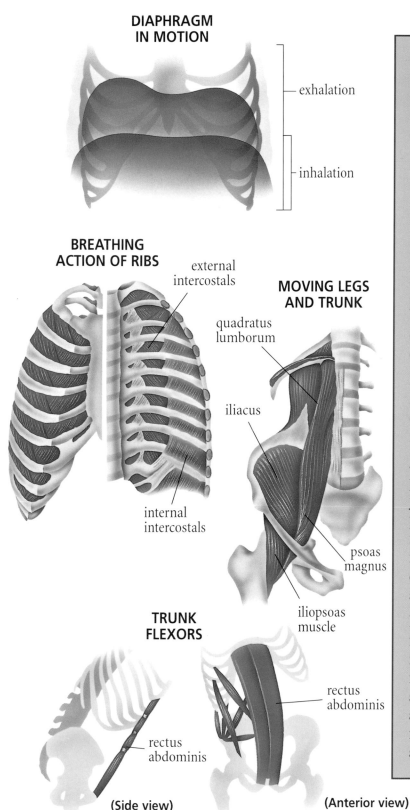

**DIAPHRAGM
IN MOTION**

exhalation

inhalation

**BREATHING
ACTION OF RIBS**

external
intercostals

internal
intercostals

**MOVING LEGS
AND TRUNK**

quadratus
lumborum

iliacus

psoas
magnus

iliopsoas
muscle

**TRUNK
FLEXORS**

rectus
abdominis

rectus
abdominis

(Side view)

(Anterior view)

Diaphragm. Ribs slant downward at rest. During inhalation, rib muscles lift the ribs to enlarge the thoracic cage and draw air into the lungs. During exhalation, the relaxing thorax pushes air out of the lungs.

The diaphragm is a major respiratory muscle that separates the thoracic and abdominal cavities. When the diaphragm contracts, it pulls down, the ribs pull up and out, and air draws into the lungs. When the diaphragm relaxes and rises, the lungs contract and squeeze out air. The diaphragm is the main muscle during both inhalation and exhalation. The diagram shows the positions of the diaphragm during breathing.

Ribs help in breathing. The intercostal muscles help in breathing when they contract and pull the ribs upward to increase the size of the rib cage.

Muscles moving legs and trunk. The psoas magnus muscle crosses various joints to bend the trunk forward over the pelvis and to help move the leg. With the iliac muscle, it forms the iliopsoas, which is the main flexor of the thigh. The quadratus lumborum aids in exhalation and flexes the chest forward and sideways.

Flexing the trunk. The rectus muscle flexes the trunk, helped by the oblique muscles. Both external oblique and internal oblique muscles move the trunk sideways. The obliques pull the ribs down and squeeze air out of the lungs. They are needed when effort is required in such situations as childbirth or defecation.

The Bones of the Pelvis

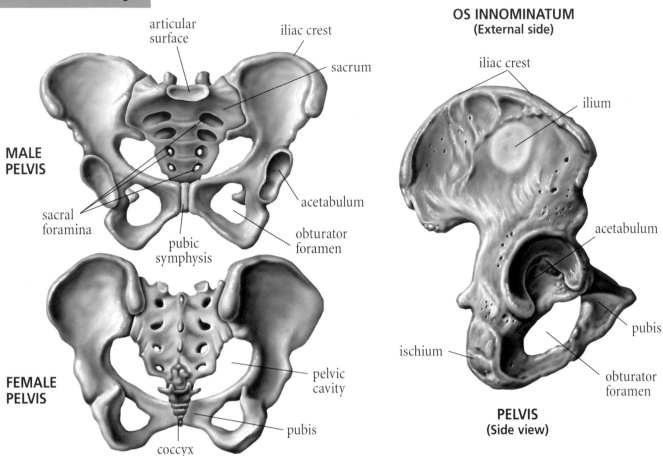

articular surface

iliac crest

sacrum

OS INNOMINATUM
(External side)

iliac crest

ilium

MALE PELVIS

acetabulum

sacral foramina

pubic symphysis

obturator foramen

acetabulum

pubis

ischium

FEMALE PELVIS

pelvic cavity

obturator foramen

pubis

PELVIS
(Side view)

coccyx

A basis for walking. The lower limbs start with the pelvis, formed by the union of the os innominatum (or coxa), the sacrum, and the coccyx.

The side of the pelvis, the os innominatum, results from the fusion of three different bones: the ilium, the ischium, and the pubis. Each side has an acetabulum, a deep socket for the head of the femur.

The ilium is a flat bone that has a smooth internal face. Its external face is rough, which increases the attachment surface for powerful muscles.

The ischium is divided into body and ramus. It has a thick upper part that belongs to the acetabulum. Its lower part is continued by the pubis.

The posterior of the pubis helps form the acetabulum. Its thickest part is the body, from which comes the ramus of the pubis, attached to the ischium. The rami of the ischium and the pubis connect to complete the obturator foramen, an aperture closed by the fibrous obturator membrane.

The sacrum is the continuation of the vertebral column at the lower end. It is formed by five sacral vertebrae. The sacrum bears two vertical rows of four holes. Through each of these holes pass the sacral nerves. The base of the sacrum has a surface that articulates with the last lumbar vertebra.

Below the sacrum is the coccyx. The sides of the coccyx join the bones that form the pelvis. The space within this basin of bone is known as the pelvic cavity. In women, the pelvic cavity contains the rectum, bladder, uterus, vagina, and the reproductive organs.

The coccyx, at the bottom end of the vertebral axis, is a rudimentary bone made up of four or five fused coxal vertebrae — all that remains of a tail.

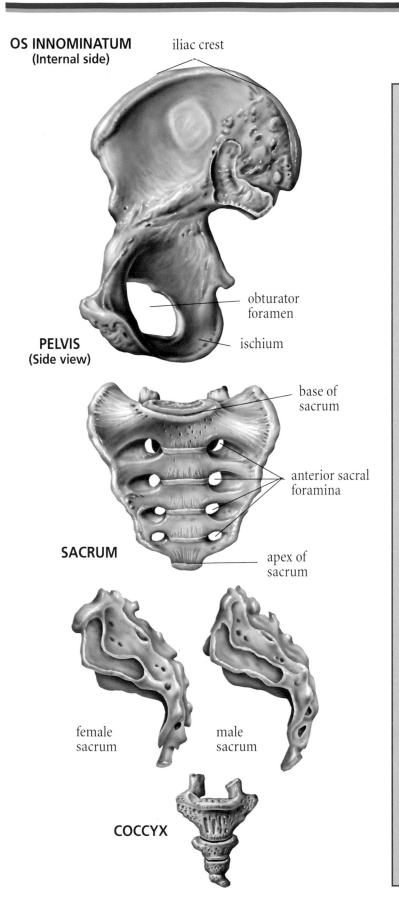

OS INNOMINATUM
(Internal side)

iliac crest

obturator foramen

PELVIS
(Side view)

ischium

base of sacrum

anterior sacral foramina

SACRUM

apex of sacrum

female sacrum

male sacrum

COCCYX

Stresses on the pelvis. The pelvis has to sustain great forces due to its location between the lower limbs and the trunk. Through the pelvis travel the shocks and pressures of both structures.

To withstand this stress from opposite directions, the joints of the pelvis are fixed, or nonmovable. The two pubis bones fit together in a joint that is called the pubic symphysis.

The os innominatum. The pelvis in women is wider and more tilted than in men. The female pelvic cavity is larger than the male's to make room for the head of a baby when giving birth. An internal view of the os innominatum, or side of the pelvis, clearly shows this birth canal.

The sacrum. The sacrum bears four pairs of openings, or foramina. These openings give access to the spinal cord. Through them pass the anterior branches of the sacral nerves and the sacral arteries.

Just as in the pelvis, there are also differences in the shape of the sacrum in both sexes. The male sacrum is longer and more fully curved. The female sacrum is wider, more sharply curved, and angled farther back to enlarge the pelvic cavity.

The joint of the sacrum and coccyx is nonmovable. It carries some very powerful ligaments to withstand the great force in transmitting the entire weight of the body to the pelvis and the lower limbs.

The coccyx. In most mammals, the vertebral column continues with up to fifty caudal, or tail, vertebrae. In humans, only four or five caudal vertebrae exist to form the coccyx. These vertebrae are fused into one bone.

The Muscles of the Pelvis

What Are They?

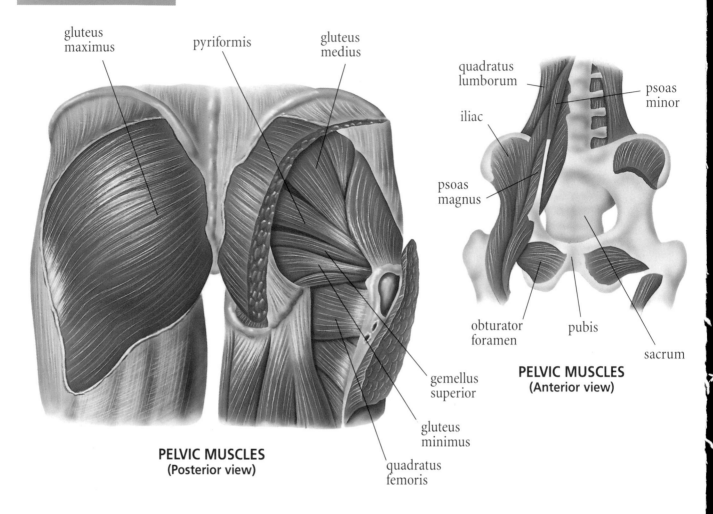

gluteus maximus

pyriformis

gluteus medius

quadratus lumborum

psoas minor

iliac

psoas magnus

obturator foramen

pubis

sacrum

PELVIC MUSCLES
(Anterior view)

gemellus superior

gluteus minimus

quadratus femoris

PELVIC MUSCLES
(Posterior view)

The anchor that helps humans move. The pelvis is important because a lot of muscles act on it, some of them being very powerful. These muscles are grouped as muscles of the lumbo-iliac region and those of the pelvic region.

The muscles of the lumbo-iliac region are the quadratus lumborum and the iliopsoas.

The quadratus lumborum is inserted into the iliac, the last rib, and the lumbar vertebrae. When this muscle contracts, it flexes the trunk sideways and keeps the pelvis level.

If the lumbar quadratus on both sides contract at the same time, they pull the last rib downward and take part in forced exhalation.

The iliopsoas has two parts: psoas and iliac. The lower end of this muscle inserts into the femur. The top of the psoas is attached to the lumbar vertebrae; the iliac binds with the iliac portion of the pelvis. The iliopsoas maintains the correct position of the pelvis. It is also the main flexor of the thigh.

The muscles of the pelvic region include the gluteus maximus, the pyriformis, the gemellus, and the quadratus femoris.

The gluteus maximus, medius, and minimus form the muscular mass of the gluteal region, which keeps the body erect. The other muscles, such as the pyriformis, the gemellus, and the quadratus femoris, function in turning the femur.

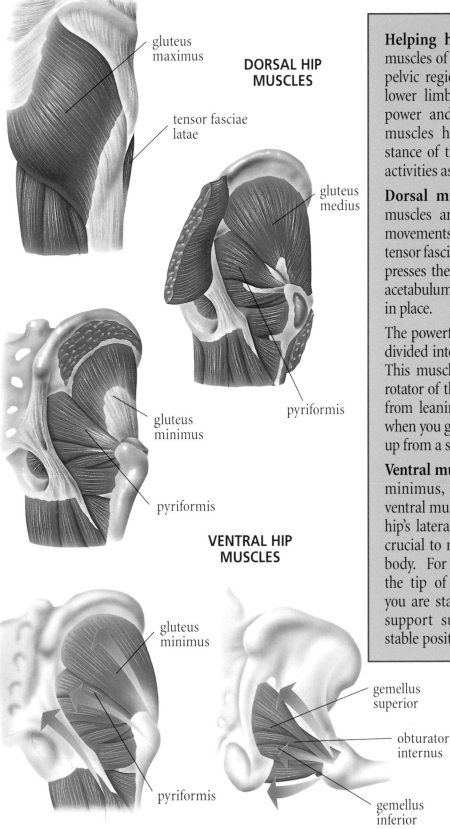

gluteus
maximus

**DORSAL HIP
MUSCLES**

tensor fasciae
latae

gluteus
medius

gluteus
minimus

pyriformis

pyriformis

**VENTRAL HIP
MUSCLES**

gluteus
minimus

pyriformis

gemellus
superior

obturator
internus

gemellus
inferior

Helping humans stay upright. The muscles of the lumbo-iliac region and the pelvic region hold the body erect on its lower limbs. This positioning involves power and coordination because these muscles have to maintain the correct stance of the body during such different activities as running, jumping, and sitting.

Dorsal muscles of the hip. Several muscles are needed to perform all the movements of the hip. For instance, the tensor fasciae latae, among other functions, presses the head of the femur against the acetabulum. This keeps the femur firmly in place.

The powerful gluteus maximus muscle is divided into a superficial and a deep part. This muscle is an outward extensor and rotator of the hip joint. It prevents the hip from leaning forward. This muscle acts when you go up stairs and when you stand up from a sitting position.

Ventral muscles of the hip. The gluteus minimus, the pyriformis, and other ventral muscles of the hip take part in the hip's lateral rotation. These muscles are crucial to maintaining the balance of the body. For instance, these muscles make the tip of the feet push forward when you are standing up. This increases the support surface and achieves a more stable position.

The Joints of the Body

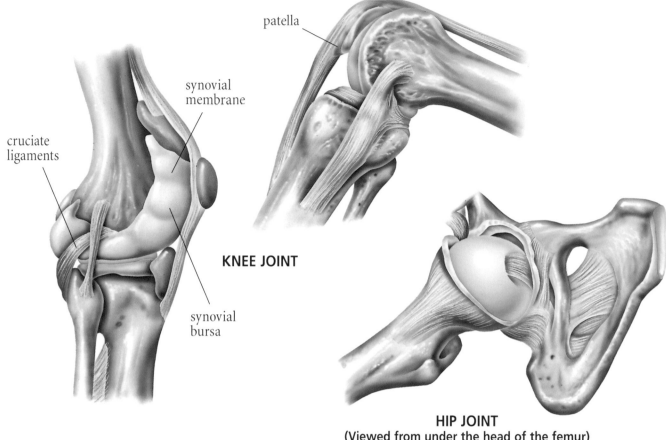

patella

synovial membrane

cruciate ligaments

KNEE JOINT

synovial bursa

HIP JOINT
(Viewed from under the head of the femur)

Types of joints. The three basic types of joints are: synarthrosis, or immovable; amphiarthrosis, or slightly movable; and diarthrosis, or freely movable.

The synarthrosis joint consists of two bones connected by a fibrous tissue that allows hardly any movement. For example, the bones of the skull are connected with the synarthrosis joint.

The amphiarthrosis joint, such as the one used between the vertebrae, allows some movement.

The diarthrosis joint allows wide movements. The hip, for example, has a ball-and-socket joint where the rounded bone end fits into a socket. This allows a great variety of movement: flexion, extension, and rotation of the leg inward and outward.

The other diarthrosis joints are: hinge, pivot, saddle, gliding, and condyloid. These six types, though shaped differently, are all synovial joints. Cartilage covers the surfaces of each joint bone, giving them a smooth surface. A strong, sleevelike sheath of fibrous connective tissue, the joint capsule, encloses the joint. Synovial membranes line the joint capsule, secreting a thick and slippery fluid that prevents friction when the bones move. The synovial fluid also nourishes the cartilage cells because most joints do not have blood vessels.

Many diarthrosis joints also have small sacs of synovial fluid, called bursae, between the joint's tendons and bones. These allow tendons to slide smoothly during joint movement. A bursa can become inflamed and painful if a joint is used excessively; this is called bursitis.

The joint capsule, the synovial membrane, ligaments, and other joint structures stabilize the joint to prevent the bones from twisting or pulling out of line.

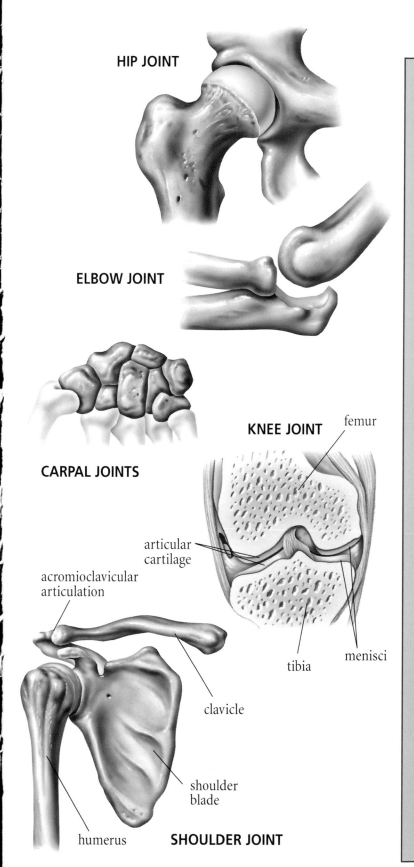

HIP JOINT

ELBOW JOINT

CARPAL JOINTS

KNEE JOINT

femur

articular cartilage

acromioclavicular articulation

tibia

menisci

clavicle

shoulder blade

humerus

SHOULDER JOINT

Connecting links. Joints enable the bones to move without friction to prevent bone wear. Several structures keep the bones in place and control their movements. Sometimes, though, trouble occurs. Arthritis is inflammation of a joint that results in pain and stiffness. Osteoarthritis is part of the aging process in which the cartilage of weight-bearing joints gradually wears away, making the surface rough. Rheumatoid arthritis, which usually starts in the extremities, involves damage of the synovial membrane.

Every joint works differently. The joint of the femur and pelvis works like a ball and socket. The humerus and ulna joint in the elbow operates like a hinge. The radio-ulnar joint acts like a pivot. In the wrist, the joints of the carpal bones are smooth and flat and move in a gliding motion.

Extra braces. Menisci are flat plates of fibro-cartilage in round, oval, triangular, or sickle shapes. They are found in the joints that are most exposed to violent jolting and frequent movement, such as the joints of the jaw, shoulder, wrist, and knee. Menisci keep the joint bones in correct position, ease gliding motions, and increase the variety of joint movements. They allow angular movement and rotation in the knee, in addition to its normal hinge movement. Menisci enable the lower jaw to open and shut and to move sideways in a grinding motion.

Strong cords. Ligaments are strong fibers that reinforce the joint between bones. They limit the kinds of independent movement possible. This prevents bones from separating from the adjacent ones.

Glossary

abdomen — the body part between the diaphragm and the pelvis.

abdominal cavity — the part of the front body cavity below the diaphragm and above the pelvic cavity.

abductor — a muscle that can lift a limb 90° upward, away from the body.

acetabulum — a cup-shaped cavity in the outside of the pelvis, into which the head of the femur fits.

actin — one of the proteins that, with myosin, make up muscle fibrils.

adductor — a muscle that moves a body part toward the midline of the body.

antagonist — something acting to oppose the action of another. Some muscles are antagonists — for example, the biceps and triceps have opposing actions.

anterior — toward the front of a human body; also called ventral.

anteversion — tipping or bending forward; forward lifting of an arm, as in pointing.

atlas — the first cervical vertebra. It supports the skull.

axis — the second cervical vertebra, forming the pivot around which the atlas, carrying the skull, moves from side to side.

calcify — to deposit calcium salts, which is part of the process of making bone.

cartilage — fibrous connective tissue found in the joints of bones. All bones are composed of cartilage until calcified.

clavicle — the bone in front of the shoulder that joins the sternum and the scapula; the collarbone.

cortex — outer layer of an organ or other body structure, such as a kidney or long bone.

diaphysis — the shaft, or central elongated part of a long bone.

dorsal — toward the back; posterior.

epiphysis — an end of a long bone.

fetus — the developing baby from the second month of pregnancy until birth.

fibula — the outer one of two long bones of the lower leg. The fibula is smaller than the tibia.

fontanels — areas of an infant's skull where the bones have not yet joined that is filled in with fibrous connective tissue.

foramen magnum — the large opening at the base of the skull through which the spinal cord joins the brain.

lamina — a thin layer, or plate.

lateral — at the side; away from the midline of the body.

ligament — a tough, cordlike structure of fibrous connective tissue that connects bone to bone.

mandible — the lower jaw.

masticate — to chew food so it can be swallowed.

medulla — the inner part of an organ, such as the kidney, that is distinct in structure and function from the cortex, or outer part.

mucosa — a membrane that secretes mucus; a lining of a body cavity that opens to the outside.

mucus — a thick liquid secreted, or produced, by mucous membrane.

muscle tone — the slight contraction always present in healthy muscles.

myofibril — one of the tiny longitudinal fibrils, which are part of a muscle fiber. Each myofibril is formed by two proteins, actin and myosin, which alternate and partly overlap each other.

myosin — one of the proteins which, together with actin, make up a myofibril.

nasal fossae — the two air cavities inside the skull that connect to the nostrils.

neurocranium — the bones of the cranium, or skull, that enclose the brain.

osseous — bony substances (spongy and compact bony tissue) that make up the hard part of bone.

ossicle — a very small bone; any of the auditory ossicles: malleus, incus, stapes.

pelvis — a basin-shaped structure at the lower end of the spine to which the upper legs are joined.

periosteum — a fibrous sheath of bone. It contains nerves and blood vessels.

posterior — toward the back; dorsal.

process — a projecting point, such as on a bone.

radius — the long bone of the forearm on the thumb side. It rotates around the ulna at the wrist.

red bone marrow — a soft substance located in the center of flat bones and at the ends of long bones. It produces blood cells, mostly erythrocytes.

retroversion — a turning back action; for example, lifting the arm backward.

sacrum — the nonmovable base of the spine, formed of five fused vertebrae.

scapula — the flat bone at the back of the shoulder that joins with the humerus bone of the upper arm.

splanchnocranium — the area of the skull that consists of the bones of the face.

tendon — a tough, cordlike structure of fibrous connective tissue that connects muscle to bone.

tibia — the larger of two lower leg bones.

ulna — the long bone of the lower arm on the side of the little finger.

ventral — toward the front; anterior.

yellow bone marrow — a soft, mostly fatty substance in the diaphysis of long bones. It strengthens bones but does not produce blood cells.

More Books to Read

The Body. Young Scientist Concepts and Projects (series). Steve Parker (Gareth Stevens)

Keeping Your Balance. Julian Rowe (Childrens)

Movement: The Muscular and Skeletal System. Jenny Bryan (Silver Burdett Press)

Muscles. Steve Parker (Milbrook Press)

Muscles and Bones. Jane Saunderson (Troll Communications)

The Musculoskeletal System. Brian Feinberg (Chelsea House)

Our Bodies. Under the Microscope (series). Casey Horton (Gareth Stevens)

Talking Bones: The Science of Forensic Anthropology. Peggy Thomas (Facts on File)

Theories of Muscle Contraction. William F. Harrington (Carolina Biological)

Understanding Your Muscles and Bones. Rebecca Treays (EDC)

The Visual Dictionary of the Skeleton. Richard Walker (DK Publications)

Videos to Watch

Bones in Action Two. (AGC Educational Media)

Bones and Muscles: A Team. (Barr Media Group)

Human Body Systems (series). (Barr Films)

I Am Joe's Foot. (Pyramid Media)

I Am Joe's Hand. (Pyramid Media)

I Am Joe's Spine. (Pyramid Media)

Web Sites to Visit

www.fitnesslink.com/changes/kidsfit.htm

www.innerbody.com/htm/body.html

kidshealth.org/kid/index.html

www.ptcentral.com/muscles/

Some web sites stay current longer than others. For further web sites, use your browsers to locate the following topics: *anatomy, biology, bones, human body, muscle system, muscles, physiology,* and *skeletal system.*

Index